50 Australian Soup
Recipes for Home

By: Kelly Johnson

Table of Contents

- Pumpkin Soup
- Pea and Ham Soup
- Seafood Chowder
- Lamb Shank Soup
- Creamy Mushroom Soup
- Tomato Soup with Basil
- Chicken and Corn Soup
- Australian Bush Tomato Soup
- Sweet Potato and Coconut Soup
- Laksa
- Potato and Leek Soup
- Beef and Vegetable Soup
- Mulligatawny Soup
- Spicy Lentil Soup
- Thai Pumpkin Soup
- Barramundi Chowder
- Kangaroo Tail Soup
- Wattleseed Soup
- Lemon Myrtle Chicken Soup
- Quandong and Chicken Soup
- Smoked Fish Chowder
- Bush Tucker Soup
- Potato Bacon Soup
- Cauliflower and Cheese Soup
- Roasted Capsicum Soup
- Garlic Prawn Soup
- Green Pea Soup
- Chilled Avocado Soup
- Emu Soup
- Lemon Asparagus Soup
- Macadamia Nut Soup
- Okra Soup
- Prawn Laksa
- Ribollita (Italian-Australian fusion)
- Spicy Sausage Soup

- Thai Coconut Chicken Soup
- Vegemite Soup
- Wild Mushroom Soup
- Chorizo and Bean Soup
- Crab Bisque
- Ginger Pumpkin Soup
- Lemon Fish Soup
- Minestrone
- Outback Oxtail Soup
- Saltbush Soup
- Thai Fish Soup
- Warrigal Greens Soup
- Zucchini and Parmesan Soup
- Lemon Chicken Soup
- Beetroot and Feta Soup

Pumpkin Soup

Ingredients:

- 1 kg pumpkin, peeled and diced
- 1 onion, diced
- 2 cloves garlic, minced
- 1 carrot, diced
- 1 potato, diced
- 4 cups vegetable or chicken broth
- 1 cup coconut milk (optional for creaminess)
- 1 tsp ground nutmeg
- Salt and pepper, to taste
- Olive oil for cooking
- Fresh parsley or chives, for garnish (optional)

Instructions:

1. Heat olive oil in a large pot over medium heat. Add diced onion and garlic, sauté until softened.
2. Add diced pumpkin, carrot, and potato to the pot. Cook for about 5 minutes, stirring occasionally.
3. Pour in the vegetable or chicken broth. Bring to a boil, then reduce heat to low. Cover and simmer for 20-25 minutes, or until the vegetables are tender.
4. Remove from heat and allow the soup to cool slightly. Use an immersion blender to puree the soup until smooth. Alternatively, transfer the soup in batches to a blender and blend until smooth. Be cautious with hot liquids in a blender.
5. Stir in coconut milk (if using), ground nutmeg, salt, and pepper to taste. Adjust seasoning as needed.
6. Serve hot, garnished with fresh parsley or chives if desired. Enjoy your delicious pumpkin soup!

This recipe is versatile, allowing for adjustments based on personal taste preferences. It's perfect for cozy evenings or as a starter for a hearty meal.

Pea and Ham Soup

Ingredients:

- 1 cup green split peas, rinsed
- 1 ham hock or ham bone (about 500g)
- 1 onion, finely chopped
- 2 carrots, diced
- 2 celery stalks, diced
- 2 cloves garlic, minced
- 1 bay leaf
- 1 tsp dried thyme
- 6 cups chicken or vegetable broth
- Salt and pepper, to taste
- Olive oil for cooking
- Fresh parsley, for garnish (optional)

Instructions:

1. Heat olive oil in a large pot over medium heat. Add chopped onion, carrots, celery, and garlic. Sauté until softened, about 5 minutes.
2. Add rinsed split peas, ham hock or bone, bay leaf, dried thyme, and chicken or vegetable broth to the pot. Bring to a boil.
3. Reduce heat to low, cover, and simmer for 1.5 to 2 hours, stirring occasionally, until the split peas are tender and the meat is falling off the bone.
4. Remove the ham hock or bone from the soup. Allow it to cool slightly, then shred the meat and discard any excess fat or bones. Return the shredded meat to the soup.
5. Season with salt and pepper to taste. If the soup is too thick, you can add more broth or water to achieve the desired consistency.
6. Serve hot, garnished with fresh parsley if desired. Enjoy your delicious pea and ham soup!

This soup is best served with crusty bread for a complete and satisfying meal.

Seafood Chowder

Ingredients:

- 500g mixed seafood (such as prawns, fish fillets, mussels, scallops), cleaned and chopped if necessary
- 1 onion, finely chopped
- 2 cloves garlic, minced
- 2 celery stalks, diced
- 2 carrots, diced
- 1 potato, diced
- 4 cups fish or seafood broth
- 1 cup heavy cream
- 2 tbsp butter
- 2 tbsp all-purpose flour
- 1 bay leaf
- 1 tsp dried thyme
- Salt and pepper, to taste
- Fresh parsley, chopped, for garnish
- Crusty bread, for serving

Instructions:

1. In a large pot, melt the butter over medium heat. Add chopped onion, garlic, celery, and carrots. Sauté until vegetables are softened, about 5-7 minutes.
2. Stir in the flour and cook for another 1-2 minutes, stirring constantly.
3. Gradually add the fish or seafood broth, stirring constantly to avoid lumps. Add the bay leaf and dried thyme. Bring to a simmer and cook for about 10 minutes, until the vegetables are tender.
4. Add diced potato to the pot and cook for another 10 minutes, or until the potato is cooked through.
5. Stir in the mixed seafood and cook for 5-7 minutes, or until the seafood is cooked through (prawns turn pink, fish flakes easily, mussels open, etc.).
6. Reduce heat to low and stir in the heavy cream. Season with salt and pepper to taste. Simmer gently for another 5 minutes to allow flavors to meld.
7. Remove the bay leaf. Serve hot, garnished with chopped fresh parsley and accompanied by crusty bread.

Enjoy your creamy and flavorful seafood chowder, perfect for a comforting meal!

Lamb Shank Soup

Ingredients:

- 2 lamb shanks
- 2 tbsp olive oil
- 1 onion, chopped
- 2 carrots, diced
- 2 celery stalks, diced
- 2 cloves garlic, minced
- 1 bay leaf
- 1 tsp dried rosemary
- 1 tsp dried thyme
- 4 cups beef or vegetable broth
- 2 cups water
- Salt and pepper, to taste
- Fresh parsley, chopped, for garnish

Instructions:

1. Heat olive oil in a large pot over medium-high heat. Season lamb shanks with salt and pepper. Brown the lamb shanks on all sides in the pot, about 4-5 minutes per side. Remove and set aside.
2. In the same pot, add chopped onion, carrots, celery, and garlic. Sauté until softened, about 5-7 minutes.
3. Return the lamb shanks to the pot. Add bay leaf, dried rosemary, dried thyme, beef or vegetable broth, and water. Bring to a boil.
4. Reduce heat to low, cover, and simmer for 2.5 to 3 hours, or until the lamb shanks are tender and falling off the bone. Skim off any foam or fat that rises to the surface during cooking.
5. Remove the lamb shanks from the soup and shred the meat using two forks, discarding any bones and excess fat.
6. Return the shredded meat to the pot. Season with salt and pepper to taste. Simmer for another 10-15 minutes to allow flavors to meld.
7. Serve hot, garnished with chopped fresh parsley.

This lamb shank soup is rich in flavor and makes a satisfying meal, especially when served with crusty bread or over mashed potatoes. Enjoy!

Creamy Mushroom Soup

Ingredients:

- 500g mushrooms, sliced (choose your favorite variety, such as button mushrooms, cremini, or portobello)
- 1 onion, chopped
- 2 cloves garlic, minced
- 4 cups vegetable or chicken broth
- 1 cup heavy cream
- 2 tbsp butter
- 2 tbsp all-purpose flour
- 1 bay leaf
- 1 tsp dried thyme
- Salt and pepper, to taste
- Fresh parsley, chopped, for garnish (optional)
- Croutons or crusty bread, for serving

Instructions:

1. In a large pot, melt the butter over medium heat. Add chopped onion and garlic, sauté until softened and fragrant, about 3-5 minutes.
2. Add sliced mushrooms to the pot. Cook, stirring occasionally, until mushrooms are softened and browned, about 8-10 minutes.
3. Sprinkle flour over the mushrooms and stir to coat evenly. Cook for another 1-2 minutes, stirring constantly.
4. Gradually add the vegetable or chicken broth, stirring constantly to avoid lumps. Add the bay leaf and dried thyme. Bring to a simmer and cook for about 10 minutes, stirring occasionally.
5. Reduce heat to low and stir in the heavy cream. Simmer gently for another 5 minutes to allow flavors to meld. Season with salt and pepper to taste.
6. Remove the bay leaf. Using an immersion blender, blend the soup until smooth. Alternatively, transfer the soup in batches to a blender and blend until smooth. Be cautious with hot liquids in a blender.
7. Serve hot, garnished with chopped fresh parsley if desired. Serve with croutons or crusty bread for dipping.

Enjoy your creamy mushroom soup, perfect for a comforting meal any time of the year!

Tomato Soup with Basil

Ingredients:

- 1.5 kg ripe tomatoes, chopped
- 1 onion, chopped
- 2 cloves garlic, minced
- 4 cups vegetable or chicken broth
- 1/4 cup fresh basil leaves, chopped
- 1/2 cup heavy cream (optional, for added creaminess)
- 2 tbsp olive oil
- 1 tbsp tomato paste
- 1 tsp sugar
- Salt and pepper, to taste
- Fresh basil leaves, for garnish
- Croutons or crusty bread, for serving

Instructions:

1. Heat olive oil in a large pot over medium heat. Add chopped onion and garlic, sauté until softened and fragrant, about 3-5 minutes.
2. Add chopped tomatoes and tomato paste to the pot. Cook, stirring occasionally, for about 10 minutes or until the tomatoes break down and release their juices.
3. Pour in the vegetable or chicken broth. Bring to a boil, then reduce heat to low. Cover and simmer for 15-20 minutes, stirring occasionally.
4. Remove from heat and allow the soup to cool slightly. Use an immersion blender to puree the soup until smooth. Alternatively, transfer the soup in batches to a blender and blend until smooth. Be cautious with hot liquids in a blender.
5. Stir in chopped fresh basil and heavy cream (if using). Season with sugar, salt, and pepper to taste. Simmer for another 5 minutes to allow flavors to meld.
6. Serve hot, garnished with fresh basil leaves and accompanied by croutons or crusty bread.

Enjoy your comforting tomato soup with basil, perfect for a cozy meal!

Chicken and Corn Soup

Ingredients:

- 2 boneless, skinless chicken breasts, thinly sliced or shredded
- 1 can (400g) creamed corn
- 1 cup corn kernels (fresh or canned)
- 1 onion, finely chopped
- 2 cloves garlic, minced
- 4 cups chicken broth
- 1 tbsp soy sauce
- 1 tbsp cornstarch, dissolved in 2 tbsp water
- 1 egg, lightly beaten
- Salt and pepper, to taste
- Spring onions, chopped, for garnish
- Sesame oil (optional), for drizzling

Instructions:

1. In a large pot, heat a bit of oil over medium heat. Add chopped onion and minced garlic, sauté until softened and fragrant, about 3-5 minutes.
2. Add thinly sliced or shredded chicken breasts to the pot. Cook until the chicken is no longer pink, about 5-7 minutes.
3. Pour in chicken broth and bring to a boil. Add creamed corn and corn kernels. Stir well.
4. Season with soy sauce, salt, and pepper to taste. Simmer for about 10 minutes, stirring occasionally.
5. Stir in the cornstarch mixture to thicken the soup. Cook for another 2-3 minutes until the soup has thickened slightly.
6. Slowly pour in the beaten egg while stirring the soup gently. This will create ribbons of egg throughout the soup.
7. Remove from heat and ladle into bowls. Garnish with chopped spring onions and drizzle with sesame oil, if desired.
8. Serve hot and enjoy your comforting chicken and corn soup!

This soup is perfect for a quick and satisfying meal, especially during colder months.

Australian Bush Tomato Soup

Ingredients:

- 1/2 cup dried bush tomatoes
- 1 onion, chopped
- 2 cloves garlic, minced
- 2 carrots, diced
- 2 celery stalks, diced
- 1 potato, diced
- 4 cups vegetable or chicken broth
- 1/2 cup heavy cream (optional, for added creaminess)
- 2 tbsp olive oil
- Salt and pepper, to taste
- Fresh parsley, chopped, for garnish

Instructions:

1. Place dried bush tomatoes in a bowl and cover with boiling water. Let them soak for about 20-30 minutes until softened. Drain and chop roughly.
2. Heat olive oil in a large pot over medium heat. Add chopped onion, garlic, carrots, and celery. Sauté until vegetables are softened, about 5-7 minutes.
3. Add diced potato and soaked bush tomatoes to the pot. Cook for another 5 minutes, stirring occasionally.
4. Pour in the vegetable or chicken broth. Bring to a boil, then reduce heat to low. Cover and simmer for 20-25 minutes, or until the vegetables are tender.
5. Remove from heat and allow the soup to cool slightly. Use an immersion blender to puree the soup until smooth. Alternatively, transfer the soup in batches to a blender and blend until smooth. Be cautious with hot liquids in a blender.
6. Stir in heavy cream (if using). Season with salt and pepper to taste. Simmer for another 5 minutes to allow flavors to meld.
7. Serve hot, garnished with chopped fresh parsley.

Enjoy your unique and flavorful Australian bush tomato soup, perfect for exploring indigenous Australian ingredients!

Sweet Potato and Coconut Soup

Ingredients:

- 2 large sweet potatoes, peeled and diced
- 1 onion, chopped
- 2 cloves garlic, minced
- 1 tbsp grated ginger
- 1 can (400ml) coconut milk
- 4 cups vegetable or chicken broth
- 2 tbsp olive oil
- 1 tsp curry powder (adjust to taste)
- Salt and pepper, to taste
- Fresh cilantro, chopped, for garnish
- Lime wedges, for serving

Instructions:

1. Heat olive oil in a large pot over medium heat. Add chopped onion, garlic, and grated ginger. Sauté until softened and fragrant, about 3-5 minutes.
2. Add diced sweet potatoes to the pot. Cook for another 5 minutes, stirring occasionally.
3. Stir in curry powder and cook for 1-2 minutes until fragrant.
4. Pour in vegetable or chicken broth and bring to a boil. Reduce heat to low, cover, and simmer for 15-20 minutes, or until sweet potatoes are tender.
5. Remove from heat and allow the soup to cool slightly. Use an immersion blender to puree the soup until smooth. Alternatively, transfer the soup in batches to a blender and blend until smooth. Be cautious with hot liquids in a blender.
6. Stir in coconut milk. Season with salt and pepper to taste. Simmer for another 5 minutes to allow flavors to meld.
7. Serve hot, garnished with chopped fresh cilantro and lime wedges on the side.

Enjoy your creamy and flavorful sweet potato and coconut soup, perfect for a cozy meal!

Laksa

Ingredients:

- 200g rice vermicelli noodles
- 400ml coconut milk
- 500ml chicken or vegetable broth
- 200g prawns, peeled and deveined
- 200g chicken breast, thinly sliced
- 1 tbsp vegetable oil
- 1 onion, finely chopped
- 2 cloves garlic, minced
- 1 tbsp grated ginger
- 2 tbsp laksa paste (store-bought or homemade)
- 1 tbsp fish sauce
- 1 tbsp soy sauce
- 1 tsp sugar
- Salt, to taste
- Fresh cilantro or Thai basil leaves, for garnish
- Lime wedges, for serving

Instructions:

1. Cook rice vermicelli noodles according to package instructions. Drain and set aside.
2. Heat vegetable oil in a large pot over medium heat. Add chopped onion, garlic, and grated ginger. Sauté until softened and fragrant, about 3-5 minutes.
3. Add laksa paste to the pot and cook for 1-2 minutes until fragrant.
4. Pour in chicken or vegetable broth and coconut milk. Bring to a boil, then reduce heat to low.
5. Add thinly sliced chicken breast to the pot. Simmer for about 5 minutes until chicken is cooked through.
6. Stir in prawns, fish sauce, soy sauce, and sugar. Cook for another 2-3 minutes until prawns are cooked and pink.
7. Season with salt to taste. Remove from heat.
8. Divide cooked rice vermicelli noodles among serving bowls. Ladle hot laksa broth with chicken and prawns over the noodles.
9. Garnish with fresh cilantro or Thai basil leaves. Serve hot with lime wedges on the side.

Enjoy your delicious and aromatic laksa, packed with vibrant flavors and perfect for a satisfying meal!

Potato and Leek Soup

Ingredients:

- 3 leeks, white and light green parts only, sliced
- 3 large potatoes, peeled and diced
- 1 onion, chopped
- 2 cloves garlic, minced
- 4 cups vegetable or chicken broth
- 1 cup heavy cream (optional, for added creaminess)
- 2 tbsp butter
- 2 tbsp olive oil
- Salt and pepper, to taste
- Fresh chives, chopped, for garnish (optional)
- Croutons or crusty bread, for serving

Instructions:

1. In a large pot, heat olive oil and butter over medium heat. Add chopped onion and garlic, sauté until softened and fragrant, about 3-5 minutes.
2. Add sliced leeks to the pot. Cook, stirring occasionally, until leeks are softened, about 5-7 minutes.
3. Add diced potatoes to the pot. Pour in vegetable or chicken broth. Bring to a boil, then reduce heat to low. Cover and simmer for 15-20 minutes, or until potatoes are tender.
4. Remove from heat and allow the soup to cool slightly. Use an immersion blender to puree the soup until smooth. Alternatively, transfer the soup in batches to a blender and blend until smooth. Be cautious with hot liquids in a blender.
5. Stir in heavy cream (if using). Season with salt and pepper to taste. Simmer for another 5 minutes to allow flavors to meld.
6. Serve hot, garnished with chopped fresh chives if desired. Serve with croutons or crusty bread on the side.

Enjoy your creamy and comforting potato and leek soup, perfect for a cozy meal any time of the year!

Beef and Vegetable Soup

Ingredients:

- 500g stewing beef, cut into bite-sized pieces
- 2 tbsp olive oil
- 1 onion, chopped
- 2 carrots, diced
- 2 celery stalks, diced
- 2 potatoes, peeled and diced
- 1 cup green beans, trimmed and cut into pieces
- 4 cups beef broth
- 1 can (400g) diced tomatoes
- 2 cloves garlic, minced
- 1 tsp dried thyme
- 1 tsp dried rosemary
- Salt and pepper, to taste
- Fresh parsley, chopped, for garnish

Instructions:

1. In a large pot, heat olive oil over medium-high heat. Add stewing beef and cook until browned on all sides, about 5-7 minutes. Remove beef from pot and set aside.
2. In the same pot, add chopped onion, carrots, and celery. Sauté until softened, about 5 minutes.
3. Add minced garlic, dried thyme, and dried rosemary to the pot. Cook for 1 minute until fragrant.
4. Return browned beef to the pot. Pour in beef broth and diced tomatoes with their juices. Bring to a boil, then reduce heat to low. Cover and simmer for 1.5 to 2 hours, or until beef is tender.
5. Add diced potatoes and green beans to the pot. Simmer for another 20-30 minutes, or until vegetables are tender.
6. Season with salt and pepper to taste. Adjust seasoning as needed.
7. Serve hot, garnished with chopped fresh parsley.

Enjoy your hearty and comforting beef and vegetable soup, perfect for a satisfying meal!

Mulligatawny Soup

Ingredients:

- 1 tbsp vegetable oil
- 1 onion, finely chopped
- 2 carrots, diced
- 2 celery stalks, diced
- 1 apple, peeled, cored, and diced
- 2 cloves garlic, minced
- 1 tbsp curry powder
- 1/2 tsp ground cumin
- 1/2 tsp ground coriander
- 1/4 tsp cayenne pepper (optional, adjust to taste)
- 1 cup red lentils, rinsed
- 4 cups chicken or vegetable broth
- 1 can (400ml) coconut milk
- 1 tbsp lemon juice
- Salt and pepper, to taste
- Fresh cilantro or parsley, chopped, for garnish

Instructions:

1. Heat vegetable oil in a large pot over medium heat. Add chopped onion, carrots, and celery. Sauté until softened, about 5 minutes.
2. Add diced apple and minced garlic to the pot. Cook for another 2-3 minutes until fragrant.
3. Stir in curry powder, ground cumin, ground coriander, and cayenne pepper (if using). Cook for 1-2 minutes until spices are toasted and fragrant.
4. Add rinsed red lentils and chicken or vegetable broth to the pot. Bring to a boil, then reduce heat to low. Cover and simmer for 20-25 minutes, or until lentils are tender.
5. Stir in coconut milk and lemon juice. Simmer for another 5 minutes to allow flavors to meld.
6. Remove from heat. Use an immersion blender to blend the soup until smooth. Alternatively, transfer the soup in batches to a blender and blend until smooth. Be cautious with hot liquids in a blender.
7. Season with salt and pepper to taste. Adjust seasoning as needed.
8. Serve hot, garnished with chopped fresh cilantro or parsley.

Enjoy your flavorful and comforting Mulligatawny soup, perfect for a warming meal!

Spicy Lentil Soup

Ingredients:

- 1 cup dried lentils (brown or green), rinsed and drained
- 1 onion, chopped
- 2 carrots, diced
- 2 celery stalks, diced
- 2 cloves garlic, minced
- 1 can (400g) diced tomatoes
- 4 cups vegetable or chicken broth
- 1 tbsp tomato paste
- 1 tsp ground cumin
- 1 tsp ground coriander
- 1/2 tsp smoked paprika
- 1/4 tsp cayenne pepper (adjust to taste)
- Salt and pepper, to taste
- 2 tbsp olive oil
- Fresh cilantro or parsley, chopped, for garnish
- Lemon wedges, for serving

Instructions:

1. Heat olive oil in a large pot over medium heat. Add chopped onion, carrots, and celery. Sauté until softened, about 5 minutes.
2. Add minced garlic, ground cumin, ground coriander, smoked paprika, and cayenne pepper (if using). Cook for 1-2 minutes until fragrant.
3. Stir in tomato paste and cook for another minute.
4. Add rinsed lentils, diced tomatoes with their juices, and vegetable or chicken broth to the pot. Bring to a boil.
5. Reduce heat to low, cover, and simmer for 25-30 minutes, or until lentils are tender.
6. Season with salt and pepper to taste. Adjust seasoning as needed.
7. Serve hot, garnished with chopped fresh cilantro or parsley. Serve with lemon wedges on the side for squeezing over the soup.

Enjoy your spicy lentil soup, perfect for a comforting and nutritious meal!

Thai Pumpkin Soup

Ingredients:

- 1 tbsp vegetable oil
- 1 onion, chopped
- 2 cloves garlic, minced
- 1 tbsp fresh ginger, grated
- 1 tbsp Thai red curry paste
- 1 kg pumpkin, peeled, seeded, and diced
- 4 cups vegetable or chicken broth
- 1 can (400ml) coconut milk
- 1 tbsp fish sauce
- 1 tbsp soy sauce
- 1 tbsp brown sugar
- Juice of 1 lime
- Salt and pepper, to taste
- Fresh cilantro, chopped, for garnish
- Red chili flakes or fresh chili slices, for garnish (optional)

Instructions:

1. Heat vegetable oil in a large pot over medium heat. Add chopped onion, minced garlic, and grated ginger. Sauté until softened and fragrant, about 3-5 minutes.
2. Stir in Thai red curry paste and cook for 1-2 minutes until fragrant.
3. Add diced pumpkin to the pot. Cook for another 5 minutes, stirring occasionally.
4. Pour in vegetable or chicken broth and bring to a boil. Reduce heat to low, cover, and simmer for 15-20 minutes, or until pumpkin is tender.
5. Remove from heat and allow the soup to cool slightly. Use an immersion blender to puree the soup until smooth. Alternatively, transfer the soup in batches to a blender and blend until smooth. Be cautious with hot liquids in a blender.
6. Stir in coconut milk, fish sauce, soy sauce, brown sugar, and lime juice. Simmer for another 5 minutes to allow flavors to meld.
7. Season with salt and pepper to taste.
8. Serve hot, garnished with chopped fresh cilantro and red chili flakes or fresh chili slices (if using).

Enjoy your creamy and flavorful Thai pumpkin soup, perfect for a comforting meal with a Thai twist!

Barramundi Chowder

Ingredients:

- 500g barramundi fillets, skin removed and cut into chunks
- 2 tbsp butter
- 1 onion, finely chopped
- 2 celery stalks, diced
- 2 carrots, diced
- 2 potatoes, peeled and diced
- 2 cloves garlic, minced
- 4 cups fish or vegetable broth
- 1 cup heavy cream
- 1/2 cup milk
- 2 tbsp all-purpose flour
- 1 bay leaf
- 1 tsp dried thyme
- Salt and pepper, to taste
- Fresh parsley, chopped, for garnish

Instructions:

1. In a large pot, melt butter over medium heat. Add chopped onion, celery, carrots, and garlic. Sauté until softened, about 5 minutes.
2. Sprinkle flour over the vegetables and stir to coat evenly. Cook for 1-2 minutes to remove the raw flour taste.
3. Gradually pour in fish or vegetable broth, stirring constantly to avoid lumps. Add bay leaf and dried thyme. Bring to a boil, then reduce heat to low.
4. Add diced potatoes to the pot. Cover and simmer for 10-15 minutes, or until potatoes are tender.
5. Stir in heavy cream and milk. Simmer for another 5 minutes.
6. Add barramundi chunks to the pot. Cook for 5-7 minutes, or until fish is cooked through and flakes easily with a fork.
7. Season with salt and pepper to taste.
8. Remove bay leaf and discard.
9. Serve hot, garnished with chopped fresh parsley.

Enjoy your delicious and creamy Barramundi chowder, perfect for a comforting seafood meal!

Kangaroo Tail Soup

Ingredients:

- 1 kangaroo tail, cut into sections
- 2 onions, chopped
- 2 carrots, diced
- 2 celery stalks, diced
- 2 potatoes, peeled and diced
- 2 cloves garlic, minced
- 4 cups beef broth
- 4 cups water
- 2 bay leaves
- 1 tsp dried thyme
- Salt and pepper, to taste
- Fresh parsley, chopped, for garnish

Instructions:

1. In a large pot, place kangaroo tail sections and cover with water. Bring to a boil over medium-high heat. Boil for 5 minutes, then drain and rinse the kangaroo tail sections.
2. In the same pot, heat a bit of oil over medium heat. Add chopped onions, carrots, celery, and minced garlic. Sauté until softened, about 5 minutes.
3. Return the kangaroo tail sections to the pot. Pour in beef broth and water. Add bay leaves and dried thyme.
4. Bring to a boil, then reduce heat to low. Cover and simmer for 3-4 hours, or until the kangaroo tail is tender and falls off the bone.
5. Remove kangaroo tail sections from the pot and let them cool slightly. Remove meat from the bones and shred into bite-sized pieces. Discard bones and return meat to the pot.
6. Add diced potatoes to the pot. Simmer for another 15-20 minutes, or until potatoes are tender.
7. Season with salt and pepper to taste.
8. Serve hot, garnished with chopped fresh parsley.

Enjoy your hearty and traditional kangaroo tail soup, a unique taste of Australian cuisine!

Wattleseed Soup

Ingredients:

- 2 tbsp wattleseed, roasted and ground
- 1 onion, chopped
- 2 carrots, diced
- 2 celery stalks, diced
- 2 potatoes, peeled and diced
- 2 cloves garlic, minced
- 4 cups vegetable or chicken broth
- 1 cup milk or cream
- 2 tbsp olive oil
- Salt and pepper, to taste
- Fresh parsley, chopped, for garnish

Instructions:

1. Heat olive oil in a large pot over medium heat. Add chopped onion, carrots, celery, and minced garlic. Sauté until softened, about 5 minutes.
2. Stir in roasted and ground wattleseed. Cook for 1-2 minutes until fragrant.
3. Add diced potatoes to the pot. Pour in vegetable or chicken broth. Bring to a boil, then reduce heat to low. Cover and simmer for 15-20 minutes, or until potatoes are tender.
4. Remove from heat and allow the soup to cool slightly. Use an immersion blender to puree the soup until smooth. Alternatively, transfer the soup in batches to a blender and blend until smooth. Be cautious with hot liquids in a blender.
5. Stir in milk or cream. Season with salt and pepper to taste. Simmer for another 5 minutes to allow flavors to meld.
6. Serve hot, garnished with chopped fresh parsley.

Enjoy your flavorful and unique wattleseed soup, celebrating indigenous Australian ingredients!

Lemon Myrtle Chicken Soup

Ingredients:

- 2 boneless, skinless chicken breasts, thinly sliced or shredded
- 1 onion, finely chopped
- 2 carrots, diced
- 2 celery stalks, diced
- 2 potatoes, peeled and diced
- 2 cloves garlic, minced
- 4 cups chicken broth
- 1 cup water
- 2 tbsp olive oil
- 2 tbsp lemon myrtle leaves, dried and crushed (or 1-2 tbsp lemon myrtle spice blend)
- Juice of 1 lemon
- Salt and pepper, to taste
- Fresh parsley, chopped, for garnish

Instructions:

1. In a large pot, heat olive oil over medium heat. Add chopped onion, carrots, celery, and minced garlic. Sauté until softened, about 5 minutes.
2. Add thinly sliced or shredded chicken breasts to the pot. Cook until chicken is no longer pink, about 5-7 minutes.
3. Stir in lemon myrtle leaves or lemon myrtle spice blend. Cook for another minute until fragrant.
4. Pour in chicken broth and water. Bring to a boil, then reduce heat to low. Cover and simmer for 15-20 minutes, or until vegetables are tender and chicken is cooked through.
5. Stir in lemon juice. Season with salt and pepper to taste. Simmer for another 5 minutes to allow flavors to meld.
6. Serve hot, garnished with chopped fresh parsley.

Enjoy your flavorful and aromatic lemon myrtle chicken soup, perfect for a comforting and satisfying meal!

Quandong and Chicken Soup

Ingredients:

- 2 chicken breasts, diced
- 1 onion, finely chopped
- 2 carrots, diced
- 2 celery stalks, diced
- 2 potatoes, peeled and diced
- 1 cup quandong, dried and chopped
- 4 cups chicken broth
- 1 cup water
- 2 tbsp olive oil
- Salt and pepper, to taste
- Fresh parsley, chopped, for garnish

Instructions:

1. In a large pot, heat olive oil over medium heat. Add chopped onion, carrots, celery, and diced chicken breasts. Sauté until chicken is no longer pink and vegetables are softened, about 5-7 minutes.
2. Stir in chopped quandong and cook for another 2-3 minutes.
3. Pour in chicken broth and water. Bring to a boil, then reduce heat to low. Cover and simmer for 20-25 minutes, or until chicken is cooked through and vegetables are tender.
4. Season with salt and pepper to taste.
5. Serve hot, garnished with chopped fresh parsley.

Enjoy your unique and flavorful quandong and chicken soup, showcasing native Australian ingredients!

Smoked Fish Chowder

Ingredients:

- 500g smoked fish fillets (such as haddock or cod), skin removed and flaked
- 2 tbsp butter
- 1 onion, finely chopped
- 2 celery stalks, diced
- 2 carrots, diced
- 2 potatoes, peeled and diced
- 2 cloves garlic, minced
- 4 cups fish or vegetable broth
- 1 cup milk or cream
- 1/2 cup white wine (optional)
- 2 tbsp all-purpose flour
- 1 bay leaf
- 1 tsp dried thyme
- Salt and pepper, to taste
- Fresh parsley, chopped, for garnish

Instructions:

1. In a large pot, melt butter over medium heat. Add chopped onion, celery, carrots, and minced garlic. Sauté until softened, about 5 minutes.
2. Sprinkle flour over the vegetables and stir to coat evenly. Cook for 1-2 minutes to remove the raw flour taste.
3. Gradually pour in fish or vegetable broth, stirring constantly to avoid lumps. Add bay leaf and dried thyme. Bring to a boil, then reduce heat to low.
4. Add diced potatoes to the pot. Cover and simmer for 10-15 minutes, or until potatoes are tender.
5. Stir in milk or cream and white wine (if using). Simmer for another 5 minutes.
6. Add flaked smoked fish to the pot. Cook for 5-7 minutes, or until fish is heated through.
7. Season with salt and pepper to taste.
8. Remove bay leaf and discard.
9. Serve hot, garnished with chopped fresh parsley.

Enjoy your delicious and creamy smoked fish chowder, perfect for a comforting meal!

Bush Tucker Soup

Ingredients:

- 1 onion, finely chopped
- 2 carrots, diced
- 2 celery stalks, diced
- 2 potatoes, peeled and diced
- 2 cloves garlic, minced
- 4 cups vegetable or chicken broth
- 1 cup water
- 1 cup wattleseed, roasted and ground (or 2 tbsp wattleseed spice blend)
- 1 cup quandong, dried and chopped
- 1 cup wild greens (such as warrigal greens or spinach), chopped
- Salt and pepper, to taste
- 2 tbsp olive oil
- Fresh herbs (such as parsley or coriander), chopped, for garnish

Instructions:

1. Heat olive oil in a large pot over medium heat. Add chopped onion, carrots, celery, and minced garlic. Sauté until softened, about 5 minutes.
2. Stir in roasted and ground wattleseed (or wattleseed spice blend). Cook for 1-2 minutes until fragrant.
3. Add diced potatoes to the pot. Pour in vegetable or chicken broth and water. Bring to a boil, then reduce heat to low. Cover and simmer for 15-20 minutes, or until potatoes are tender.
4. Stir in chopped quandong and wild greens (such as warrigal greens or spinach). Simmer for another 5 minutes.
5. Season with salt and pepper to taste.
6. Serve hot, garnished with chopped fresh herbs.

Notes:

- **Wattleseed**: Wattleseed adds a nutty, roasted flavor. If using whole wattleseed, roast it first in a dry pan over medium heat until fragrant, then grind it.
- **Quandong**: Dried quandong adds a tangy and slightly sweet flavor to the soup. It's a native Australian fruit often used in bush tucker cuisine.
- **Wild Greens**: Warrigal greens or other wild greens provide a nutritious addition with a unique taste.

Enjoy your bush tucker soup, embracing the flavors and ingredients of Aboriginal Australian cuisine! Adjust the ingredients based on availability and personal taste preferences for a delightful experience.

Potato Bacon Soup

Ingredients:

- 6 slices bacon, chopped
- 1 onion, chopped
- 2 cloves garlic, minced
- 4 cups potatoes, peeled and diced
- 3 cups chicken broth
- 1 cup milk
- 1/2 cup heavy cream (optional, for extra richness)
- 1/2 cup shredded cheddar cheese (optional, for garnish)
- Salt and pepper, to taste
- Fresh chives or green onions, chopped, for garnish

Instructions:

1. In a large pot or Dutch oven, cook chopped bacon over medium heat until crispy. Remove bacon with a slotted spoon and set aside on a paper towel-lined plate.
2. In the same pot with bacon drippings, add chopped onion and minced garlic. Sauté until onion is translucent and garlic is fragrant, about 3-4 minutes.
3. Add diced potatoes to the pot and stir to coat with the bacon fat and onion mixture. Cook for 2-3 minutes.
4. Pour in chicken broth and bring to a boil. Reduce heat to medium-low and simmer, covered, for 15-20 minutes, or until potatoes are tender.
5. Use an immersion blender to blend the soup until smooth and creamy. Alternatively, transfer half of the soup to a blender and blend until smooth, then return to the pot.
6. Stir in milk and heavy cream (if using). Season with salt and pepper to taste.
7. Serve hot, garnished with chopped crispy bacon, shredded cheddar cheese (if desired), and fresh chives or green onions.

Enjoy your comforting and delicious potato bacon soup! It's perfect for a cozy meal any time of the year.

Cauliflower and Cheese Soup

Ingredients:

- 1 head cauliflower, chopped into florets
- 1 onion, chopped
- 2 cloves garlic, minced
- 4 cups vegetable or chicken broth
- 1 cup milk or cream
- 2 cups shredded cheddar cheese (or any cheese of your choice)
- 2 tbsp butter
- 2 tbsp all-purpose flour
- Salt and pepper, to taste
- Fresh chives or parsley, chopped, for garnish

Instructions:

1. In a large pot, melt butter over medium heat. Add chopped onion and minced garlic. Sauté until onion is translucent and garlic is fragrant, about 3-4 minutes.
2. Stir in chopped cauliflower florets. Cook for another 5 minutes, stirring occasionally.
3. Sprinkle flour over the cauliflower mixture and stir to coat evenly. Cook for 1-2 minutes to remove the raw flour taste.
4. Gradually pour in vegetable or chicken broth, stirring constantly to avoid lumps. Bring to a boil, then reduce heat to medium-low. Cover and simmer for 15-20 minutes, or until cauliflower is tender.
5. Use an immersion blender to blend the soup until smooth and creamy. Alternatively, transfer half of the soup to a blender and blend until smooth, then return to the pot.
6. Stir in milk or cream and shredded cheddar cheese. Continue stirring until the cheese is melted and the soup is smooth.
7. Season with salt and pepper to taste.
8. Serve hot, garnished with chopped fresh chives or parsley.

Enjoy your creamy and flavorful cauliflower and cheese soup! It's a satisfying dish that's sure to warm you up.

Roasted Capsicum Soup

Ingredients:

- 4 red bell peppers
- 2 tbsp olive oil
- 1 onion, chopped
- 2 cloves garlic, minced
- 1 potato, peeled and diced
- 4 cups vegetable or chicken broth
- 1/2 cup heavy cream (optional, for extra creaminess)
- Salt and pepper, to taste
- Fresh basil or parsley, chopped, for garnish

Instructions:

1. Preheat your oven to 200°C (400°F). Place whole red bell peppers on a baking sheet and roast in the oven for 20-25 minutes, or until the skins are charred and blistered, turning occasionally.
2. Remove the roasted peppers from the oven and immediately transfer them to a bowl. Cover the bowl with plastic wrap or a kitchen towel and let them steam for about 10 minutes. This will make it easier to peel off the skins.
3. Once cooled, peel off the charred skins of the peppers, remove the seeds and membranes, and roughly chop the flesh.
4. In a large pot, heat olive oil over medium heat. Add chopped onion and minced garlic. Sauté until onion is translucent and garlic is fragrant, about 3-4 minutes.
5. Add diced potato and chopped roasted bell peppers to the pot. Cook for another 5 minutes, stirring occasionally.
6. Pour in vegetable or chicken broth. Bring to a boil, then reduce heat to medium-low. Cover and simmer for 15-20 minutes, or until potatoes are tender.
7. Use an immersion blender to blend the soup until smooth and creamy. Alternatively, transfer half of the soup to a blender and blend until smooth, then return to the pot.
8. Stir in heavy cream (if using). Season with salt and pepper to taste.
9. Serve hot, garnished with chopped fresh basil or parsley.

Enjoy your delicious and vibrant roasted capsicum soup! It's perfect as a starter or a light meal, especially during cooler weather.

Garlic Prawn Soup

Ingredients:

- 300g prawns, peeled and deveined
- 2 tbsp olive oil
- 4 cloves garlic, minced
- 1 onion, finely chopped
- 2 celery stalks, diced
- 1 carrot, diced
- 1 red bell pepper, diced
- 4 cups fish or vegetable broth
- 1 cup coconut milk
- 1 tbsp fish sauce
- 1 tsp soy sauce
- 1 tsp chili flakes (optional, adjust to taste)
- Salt and pepper, to taste
- Fresh coriander or parsley, chopped, for garnish
- Lime wedges, for serving

Instructions:

1. Heat olive oil in a large pot over medium heat. Add minced garlic and chopped onion. Sauté until onion is translucent and garlic is fragrant, about 3-4 minutes.
2. Add diced celery, carrot, and red bell pepper to the pot. Sauté for another 5 minutes, stirring occasionally.
3. Pour in fish or vegetable broth. Bring to a boil, then reduce heat to medium-low. Cover and simmer for 10 minutes, or until vegetables are tender.
4. Stir in coconut milk, fish sauce, soy sauce, and chili flakes (if using). Simmer for another 5 minutes to allow flavors to meld.
5. Add peeled and deveined prawns to the pot. Cook for 3-4 minutes, or until prawns are pink and cooked through.
6. Season with salt and pepper to taste.
7. Serve hot, garnished with chopped fresh coriander or parsley. Serve with lime wedges on the side for squeezing over the soup.

Enjoy your aromatic and delicious garlic prawn soup! It's perfect for showcasing the flavors of seafood with a touch of spice and coconut milk richness.

Green Pea Soup

Ingredients:

- 2 cups frozen green peas
- 1 onion, chopped
- 2 cloves garlic, minced
- 2 tbsp butter or olive oil
- 4 cups vegetable or chicken broth
- 1/2 cup milk or cream
- Salt and pepper, to taste
- Fresh mint leaves, chopped (optional, for garnish)

Instructions:

1. In a large pot, melt butter or heat olive oil over medium heat. Add chopped onion and minced garlic. Sauté until onion is translucent and garlic is fragrant, about 3-4 minutes.
2. Add frozen green peas to the pot. Cook for another 2-3 minutes, stirring occasionally.
3. Pour in vegetable or chicken broth. Bring to a boil, then reduce heat to medium-low. Cover and simmer for 10-15 minutes, or until peas are tender.
4. Use an immersion blender to blend the soup until smooth and creamy. Alternatively, transfer half of the soup to a blender and blend until smooth, then return to the pot.
5. Stir in milk or cream. Season with salt and pepper to taste.
6. Serve hot, garnished with chopped fresh mint leaves if desired.

Enjoy your creamy and flavorful green pea soup! It's a wonderful way to enjoy the sweetness of peas in a comforting soup.

Chilled Avocado Soup

Ingredients:

- 2 ripe avocados, peeled and pitted
- 1 cucumber, peeled and chopped
- 1/2 cup plain Greek yogurt
- 1/4 cup fresh cilantro or parsley leaves
- 1 garlic clove, minced
- Juice of 1 lime
- 2 cups vegetable or chicken broth, chilled
- Salt and pepper, to taste
- Optional garnishes: diced avocado, chopped cilantro or parsley, crumbled feta cheese, drizzle of olive oil

Instructions:

1. In a blender or food processor, combine ripe avocados, chopped cucumber, Greek yogurt, fresh cilantro or parsley leaves, minced garlic, and lime juice.
2. Blend until smooth and creamy.
3. Gradually add chilled vegetable or chicken broth, blending until desired consistency is reached. You may need to adjust the amount of broth depending on how thick or thin you prefer your soup.
4. Season with salt and pepper to taste.
5. Transfer the soup to a bowl or container and refrigerate for at least 1 hour to chill.
6. Before serving, taste and adjust seasoning if needed.
7. Serve chilled avocado soup in bowls, garnished with diced avocado, chopped cilantro or parsley, crumbled feta cheese, and a drizzle of olive oil if desired.

Enjoy your refreshing and creamy chilled avocado soup! It's a delightful way to enjoy the creamy texture and mild flavor of avocados, especially during warmer weather.

Emu Soup

Ingredients:

- 500g emu meat, diced (you can use emu fillet or other cuts)
- 2 tbsp olive oil
- 1 onion, finely chopped
- 2 carrots, diced
- 2 celery stalks, diced
- 2 potatoes, peeled and diced
- 2 cloves garlic, minced
- 4 cups beef or vegetable broth
- 1 cup water
- 1/2 cup red wine (optional)
- 1 bay leaf
- 1 tsp dried thyme
- Salt and pepper, to taste
- Fresh parsley, chopped, for garnish

Instructions:

1. In a large pot, heat olive oil over medium heat. Add diced emu meat and brown on all sides, about 5-7 minutes. Remove emu meat from the pot and set aside.
2. In the same pot, add chopped onion, carrots, celery, and minced garlic. Sauté until vegetables are softened, about 5 minutes.
3. Return the browned emu meat to the pot. Pour in beef or vegetable broth and water. Add red wine (if using), bay leaf, and dried thyme. Bring to a boil.
4. Reduce heat to low, cover, and simmer for 1 to 1.5 hours, or until emu meat is tender.
5. Add diced potatoes to the pot and simmer for another 15-20 minutes, or until potatoes are cooked through.
6. Season with salt and pepper to taste.
7. Serve hot, garnished with chopped fresh parsley.

Enjoy your hearty and flavorful emu soup! It's a great way to experience the unique taste of emu meat in a comforting and nutritious dish. Adjust the cooking time as needed to ensure the emu meat is tender and flavorful.

Lemon Asparagus Soup

Ingredients:

- 1 bunch asparagus, tough ends trimmed and chopped
- 1 onion, chopped
- 2 cloves garlic, minced
- 2 tbsp butter or olive oil
- 4 cups vegetable or chicken broth
- Zest and juice of 1 lemon
- 1/2 cup heavy cream (optional, for extra creaminess)
- Salt and pepper, to taste
- Fresh parsley or dill, chopped, for garnish

Instructions:

1. In a large pot, melt butter or heat olive oil over medium heat. Add chopped onion and minced garlic. Sauté until onion is translucent and garlic is fragrant, about 3-4 minutes.
2. Add chopped asparagus to the pot. Cook for another 5 minutes, stirring occasionally.
3. Pour in vegetable or chicken broth. Bring to a boil, then reduce heat to medium-low. Cover and simmer for 15-20 minutes, or until asparagus is tender.
4. Use an immersion blender to blend the soup until smooth and creamy. Alternatively, transfer half of the soup to a blender and blend until smooth, then return to the pot.
5. Stir in lemon zest and juice. If using, stir in heavy cream for extra creaminess.
6. Season with salt and pepper to taste.
7. Serve hot or chilled, garnished with chopped fresh parsley or dill.

Enjoy your light and tangy lemon asparagus soup! It's a perfect way to enjoy the fresh flavors of asparagus with a hint of citrus brightness.

Macadamia Nut Soup

Ingredients:

- 1 cup raw macadamia nuts
- 2 tbsp butter or olive oil
- 1 onion, chopped
- 2 cloves garlic, minced
- 2 potatoes, peeled and diced
- 4 cups vegetable or chicken broth
- 1 cup milk or cream
- Salt and pepper, to taste
- Fresh parsley or chives, chopped, for garnish

Instructions:

1. In a large pot, toast the raw macadamia nuts over medium heat until lightly browned and fragrant, about 3-4 minutes. Remove from heat and set aside.
2. In the same pot, melt butter or heat olive oil over medium heat. Add chopped onion and minced garlic. Sauté until onion is translucent and garlic is fragrant, about 3-4 minutes.
3. Add diced potatoes to the pot. Cook for another 5 minutes, stirring occasionally.
4. Pour in vegetable or chicken broth. Bring to a boil, then reduce heat to medium-low. Cover and simmer for 15-20 minutes, or until potatoes are tender.
5. Transfer the toasted macadamia nuts to a blender or food processor. Add a ladleful of the hot soup broth. Blend until smooth and creamy.
6. Pour the blended macadamia mixture back into the pot with the soup. Stir to combine.
7. Stir in milk or cream. Simmer for another 5 minutes, stirring occasionally.
8. Season with salt and pepper to taste.
9. Serve hot, garnished with chopped fresh parsley or chives.

Enjoy your creamy and nutty macadamia nut soup! It's a luxurious dish that pairs well with crusty bread or a fresh green salad. Adjust the consistency by adding more broth or cream as desired.

Okra Soup

Ingredients:

- 1 lb fresh okra, sliced (or 1 lb frozen sliced okra)
- 1 onion, chopped
- 2 cloves garlic, minced
- 2 tomatoes, chopped (or 1 can diced tomatoes)
- 1 red bell pepper, chopped
- 1 green bell pepper, chopped
- 2 cups chopped spinach or collard greens
- 1 lb chicken thighs or drumsticks, skinless and bone-in (optional)
- 4 cups chicken or vegetable broth
- 1/2 cup palm oil or vegetable oil
- 2 tbsp ground crayfish (optional)
- 1 tbsp ground cayenne pepper (adjust to taste)
- Salt and pepper, to taste
- Fresh cilantro or parsley, chopped, for garnish

Instructions:

1. If using chicken, season with salt and pepper. In a large pot, heat oil over medium heat. Add chicken and brown on all sides, about 5-7 minutes. Remove chicken from pot and set aside.
2. In the same pot, add chopped onion and minced garlic. Sauté until onion is translucent and garlic is fragrant, about 3-4 minutes.
3. Add chopped tomatoes, red bell pepper, and green bell pepper to the pot. Cook for another 5 minutes, stirring occasionally.
4. Return the browned chicken (if using) to the pot. Pour in chicken or vegetable broth. Bring to a boil, then reduce heat to medium-low. Cover and simmer for 30 minutes, or until chicken is cooked through and tender.
5. Add sliced okra and chopped spinach or collard greens to the pot. Simmer for another 15-20 minutes, or until okra is tender.
6. Stir in ground crayfish (if using), ground cayenne pepper, salt, and pepper to taste.
7. Remove from heat and let the soup rest for a few minutes to allow flavors to meld.
8. Serve hot, garnished with chopped fresh cilantro or parsley.

Enjoy your flavorful and nutritious okra soup! It pairs well with rice or fufu (a traditional West African starch) for a complete meal. Adjust the spice level and ingredients according to your taste preferences.

Prawn Laksa

Ingredients:

- 300g prawns, peeled and deveined
- 200g rice noodles (vermicelli or thick noodles)
- 1 can (400ml) coconut milk
- 4 cups chicken or vegetable broth
- 2 tbsp laksa paste (store-bought or homemade)
- 1 onion, finely chopped
- 2 cloves garlic, minced
- 1 inch piece of ginger, grated
- 1-2 tbsp fish sauce (adjust to taste)
- 1 tbsp soy sauce
- 1 tbsp brown sugar
- Juice of 1 lime
- 1 cup bean sprouts
- Fresh cilantro or Thai basil leaves, chopped, for garnish
- Hard-boiled eggs, halved (optional, for serving)

Instructions:

1. Cook rice noodles according to package instructions. Drain and set aside.
2. In a large pot or deep pan, heat a bit of oil over medium heat. Add chopped onion, minced garlic, and grated ginger. Sauté until fragrant, about 2-3 minutes.
3. Add laksa paste to the pot and stir for another minute to release its flavors.
4. Pour in chicken or vegetable broth and bring to a boil. Reduce heat to medium-low.
5. Stir in coconut milk, fish sauce, soy sauce, and brown sugar. Simmer for 10-15 minutes to allow flavors to meld together.
6. Add peeled and deveined prawns to the pot. Cook for 3-4 minutes, or until prawns are pink and cooked through.
7. Stir in lime juice.
8. To serve, divide cooked rice noodles among bowls. Ladle the hot laksa broth over the noodles. Top with bean sprouts, chopped cilantro or Thai basil leaves, and halved hard-boiled eggs if using.
9. Serve immediately and enjoy your delicious prawn laksa!

Prawn laksa is best enjoyed hot, with its aromatic coconut curry broth and tender prawns. Adjust the spiciness and seasoning according to your preference for a perfect bowl of laksa.

Ribollita (Italian-Australian fusion)

Ingredients:

- 1 onion, chopped
- 2 cloves garlic, minced
- 2 carrots, diced
- 2 celery stalks, diced
- 1 zucchini, diced
- 1 red bell pepper, diced
- 1 can (400g) cannellini beans, drained and rinsed
- 1 can (400g) diced tomatoes
- 4 cups vegetable or chicken broth
- 1 bunch kale or spinach, chopped
- 4 slices of sourdough bread, toasted and torn into pieces
- 1/4 cup grated Parmesan cheese
- 2 tbsp olive oil
- Salt and pepper, to taste
- Fresh basil or parsley, chopped, for garnish

Instructions:

1. In a large pot, heat olive oil over medium heat. Add chopped onion and minced garlic. Sauté until onion is translucent and garlic is fragrant, about 3-4 minutes.
2. Add diced carrots, celery, zucchini, and red bell pepper to the pot. Cook for another 5 minutes, stirring occasionally.
3. Stir in diced tomatoes and cannellini beans. Pour in vegetable or chicken broth. Bring to a boil, then reduce heat to medium-low. Cover and simmer for 20-25 minutes, or until vegetables are tender.
4. Stir in chopped kale or spinach. Simmer for another 5-7 minutes until greens are wilted.
5. Add torn pieces of toasted sourdough bread to the pot. Stir well to combine, allowing the bread to break down and thicken the soup.
6. Season with salt and pepper to taste.
7. Serve hot, garnished with grated Parmesan cheese and chopped fresh basil or parsley.

Enjoy your comforting and flavorful Italian-Australian fusion ribollita! The addition of sourdough bread and Parmesan cheese adds a unique twist to this traditional Tuscan soup, making it even heartier and more satisfying.

Spicy Sausage Soup

Ingredients:

- 1 lb spicy Italian sausage, casings removed
- 1 onion, chopped
- 2 cloves garlic, minced
- 2 carrots, diced
- 2 celery stalks, diced
- 1 red bell pepper, chopped
- 1 can (400g) diced tomatoes
- 4 cups chicken or vegetable broth
- 1 tsp dried thyme
- 1 tsp dried oregano
- 1/2 tsp smoked paprika
- 1/4 tsp red pepper flakes (adjust to taste)
- Salt and pepper, to taste
- 1 cup small pasta (such as macaroni or fusilli)
- Fresh parsley, chopped, for garnish

Instructions:

1. In a large pot or Dutch oven, cook the spicy Italian sausage over medium-high heat, breaking it up into small pieces with a spoon, until browned and cooked through. Remove the sausage from the pot and set aside.
2. In the same pot, add chopped onion and minced garlic. Sauté until onion is translucent and garlic is fragrant, about 3-4 minutes.
3. Add diced carrots, celery, and red bell pepper to the pot. Cook for another 5 minutes, stirring occasionally.
4. Stir in diced tomatoes (with their juices) and cooked sausage. Pour in chicken or vegetable broth. Add dried thyme, dried oregano, smoked paprika, and red pepper flakes. Season with salt and pepper to taste.
5. Bring the soup to a boil, then reduce heat to medium-low. Cover and simmer for 15-20 minutes, or until vegetables are tender.
6. Stir in small pasta and continue to simmer for another 10-12 minutes, or until pasta is al dente.
7. Taste and adjust seasoning if needed.
8. Serve hot, garnished with chopped fresh parsley.

Enjoy your hearty and spicy sausage soup! It's perfect for a comforting meal, especially during colder weather. Adjust the level of spiciness by varying the amount of red pepper flakes or using mild sausage if preferred.

Thai Coconut Chicken Soup

Ingredients:

- 1 lb boneless, skinless chicken breasts or thighs, thinly sliced
- 4 cups chicken broth
- 1 can (14 oz) coconut milk
- 1 stalk lemongrass, cut into 2-inch pieces and bruised
- 3-4 slices galangal or ginger
- 3-4 kaffir lime leaves, torn
- 1-2 red or green Thai chilies, thinly sliced (adjust to taste)
- 1 small onion, thinly sliced
- 2-3 cloves garlic, minced
- 1-2 tbsp fish sauce (adjust to taste)
- 1-2 tbsp soy sauce
- 1 tbsp brown sugar
- Juice of 1-2 limes
- 1 cup mushrooms, sliced (such as straw mushrooms or button mushrooms)
- 1 cup cherry tomatoes, halved
- Fresh cilantro leaves, chopped, for garnish
- Thai basil leaves, torn, for garnish (optional)

Instructions:

1. In a large pot, bring chicken broth to a boil over medium-high heat.
2. Add lemongrass, galangal or ginger slices, and torn kaffir lime leaves to the pot. Reduce heat to medium-low and simmer for 5-10 minutes to infuse the broth with flavors.
3. Add thinly sliced chicken to the pot. Cook until chicken is cooked through, about 5-7 minutes.
4. Stir in coconut milk, sliced Thai chilies, thinly sliced onion, minced garlic, fish sauce, soy sauce, and brown sugar. Simmer gently for another 5 minutes to blend flavors.
5. Add sliced mushrooms and halved cherry tomatoes to the pot. Simmer for another 2-3 minutes, or until mushrooms are tender.
6. Remove lemongrass stalks, galangal or ginger slices, and torn kaffir lime leaves from the soup.
7. Stir in lime juice. Taste and adjust seasoning with more fish sauce, soy sauce, or lime juice if needed.
8. Serve hot, garnished with chopped fresh cilantro leaves and torn Thai basil leaves (if using).

Enjoy your fragrant and creamy Thai Coconut Chicken Soup! It's a comforting and flavorful soup that combines the richness of coconut milk with the vibrant flavors of Thai herbs and spices. Adjust the spiciness and seasoning according to your preference for a perfect bowl of Tom Kha Gai.

Vegemite Soup

Ingredients:

- 2 tbsp butter
- 1 onion, finely chopped
- 2 carrots, diced
- 2 celery stalks, diced
- 2 potatoes, peeled and diced
- 4 cups vegetable or chicken broth
- 2 tbsp Vegemite
- 1/2 cup heavy cream or milk
- Salt and pepper, to taste
- Fresh parsley, chopped, for garnish

Instructions:

1. In a large pot, melt butter over medium heat. Add chopped onion and sauté until translucent, about 3-4 minutes.
2. Add diced carrots, celery, and potatoes to the pot. Cook for another 5 minutes, stirring occasionally.
3. Pour in vegetable or chicken broth. Bring to a boil, then reduce heat to medium-low. Cover and simmer for 15-20 minutes, or until vegetables are tender.
4. In a small bowl, dissolve Vegemite in a cup of hot water or broth to make it easier to incorporate into the soup.
5. Add the dissolved Vegemite mixture to the pot. Stir well to combine.
6. Stir in heavy cream or milk. Simmer for another 5 minutes, stirring occasionally.
7. Season with salt and pepper to taste.
8. Serve hot, garnished with chopped fresh parsley.

Enjoy your unique and savory Vegemite soup! It's a comforting dish with a distinctive Australian flavor that pairs well with crusty bread or a simple salad. Adjust the thickness by adding more broth or cream according to your preference.

Wild Mushroom Soup

Ingredients:

- 1 lb mixed wild mushrooms (such as chanterelles, shiitake, oyster mushrooms), cleaned and sliced
- 2 tbsp butter
- 1 onion, chopped
- 2 cloves garlic, minced
- 2 celery stalks, chopped
- 2 carrots, chopped
- 1 potato, peeled and diced
- 4 cups vegetable or chicken broth
- 1/2 cup dry white wine (optional)
- 1 cup heavy cream
- 2 tbsp all-purpose flour (optional, for thickening)
- Salt and pepper, to taste
- Fresh thyme or parsley, chopped, for garnish

Instructions:

1. In a large pot, melt butter over medium heat. Add chopped onion, minced garlic, chopped celery, and chopped carrots. Sauté until onion is translucent and vegetables are tender, about 5-7 minutes.
2. Add sliced wild mushrooms to the pot. Cook, stirring occasionally, until mushrooms are softened and slightly browned, about 8-10 minutes.
3. Pour in vegetable or chicken broth and optional dry white wine. Bring to a boil, then reduce heat to medium-low. Cover and simmer for 15-20 minutes, allowing flavors to meld together.
4. If using, whisk all-purpose flour into heavy cream until smooth. Stir the cream mixture into the soup, simmer for another 5 minutes to thicken slightly.
5. Season with salt and pepper to taste.
6. Remove from heat and let the soup cool slightly.
7. Use an immersion blender to blend the soup until smooth. Alternatively, transfer half of the soup to a blender and blend until smooth, then return to the pot.
8. Serve hot, garnished with chopped fresh thyme or parsley.

Enjoy your creamy and flavorful wild mushroom soup! It's perfect as a starter or a comforting main dish, especially during cooler months when wild mushrooms are in season. Adjust the types of mushrooms used according to availability and personal preference for a unique variation each time you make it.

Chorizo and Bean Soup

Ingredients:

- 1 lb chorizo sausage, casings removed and sliced
- 1 onion, chopped
- 2 cloves garlic, minced
- 2 carrots, diced
- 2 celery stalks, diced
- 1 red bell pepper, diced
- 2 cans (15 oz each) beans (such as cannellini beans or kidney beans), drained and rinsed
- 4 cups chicken or vegetable broth
- 1 can (14 oz) diced tomatoes
- 1 tsp smoked paprika
- 1/2 tsp ground cumin
- Salt and pepper, to taste
- Fresh parsley or cilantro, chopped, for garnish

Instructions:

1. In a large pot or Dutch oven, cook the sliced chorizo sausage over medium-high heat until browned and cooked through, breaking it up into smaller pieces with a spoon. Remove sausage from the pot and set aside.
2. In the same pot, add chopped onion and minced garlic. Sauté until onion is translucent and garlic is fragrant, about 3-4 minutes.
3. Add diced carrots, celery, and red bell pepper to the pot. Cook for another 5 minutes, stirring occasionally.
4. Stir in drained and rinsed beans, diced tomatoes (with their juices), and cooked chorizo sausage.
5. Pour in chicken or vegetable broth. Add smoked paprika, ground cumin, salt, and pepper to taste. Stir well to combine.
6. Bring the soup to a boil, then reduce heat to medium-low. Cover and simmer for 20-25 minutes, or until vegetables are tender and flavors have melded together.
7. Taste and adjust seasoning if needed.
8. Serve hot, garnished with chopped fresh parsley or cilantro.

Enjoy your delicious chorizo and bean soup! It's a comforting and satisfying meal, perfect for chilly days. The spicy chorizo adds a robust flavor that complements the creamy beans and savory broth beautifully.

Crab Bisque

Ingredients:

- 1 lb crab meat (fresh or canned), picked over for shells
- 4 tbsp unsalted butter
- 1 onion, finely chopped
- 2 celery stalks, finely chopped
- 2 carrots, finely chopped
- 2 cloves garlic, minced
- 1/4 cup all-purpose flour
- 4 cups seafood or chicken broth
- 1 cup heavy cream
- 1/4 cup dry sherry (optional)
- 1 tsp Old Bay seasoning (or to taste)
- Salt and pepper, to taste
- Fresh parsley, chopped, for garnish

Instructions:

1. In a large pot or Dutch oven, melt butter over medium heat. Add chopped onion, celery, and carrots. Sauté until vegetables are softened, about 5-7 minutes.
2. Add minced garlic to the pot and sauté for another minute until fragrant.
3. Sprinkle flour over the vegetables and stir to combine. Cook for 2-3 minutes to cook out the raw flour taste.
4. Gradually pour in seafood or chicken broth, stirring constantly to prevent lumps from forming.
5. Add heavy cream and dry sherry (if using) to the pot. Bring to a simmer over medium heat, stirring occasionally.
6. Stir in Old Bay seasoning, salt, and pepper to taste.
7. Gently fold in the crab meat, being careful not to break up the chunks too much. Simmer for another 5-7 minutes to heat the crab meat through.
8. Taste and adjust seasoning if needed.
9. Serve hot, garnished with chopped fresh parsley.

Enjoy your creamy and flavorful crab bisque! This soup is perfect as a starter for a special meal or as a comforting dish on its own. Adjust the thickness by adding more broth or cream according to your preference.

Ginger Pumpkin Soup

Ingredients:

- 2 tbsp olive oil or butter
- 1 onion, chopped
- 2 cloves garlic, minced
- 1 tbsp fresh ginger, grated
- 1 medium pumpkin (about 3 lbs), peeled, seeded, and diced (or 2 cans of pumpkin puree)
- 4 cups vegetable or chicken broth
- 1 can (14 oz) coconut milk
- 1 tbsp honey or maple syrup (optional, to taste)
- Salt and pepper, to taste
- 1/2 tsp ground cinnamon
- 1/4 tsp ground nutmeg
- Fresh cilantro or parsley, chopped, for garnish

Instructions:

1. In a large pot or Dutch oven, heat olive oil or butter over medium heat. Add chopped onion and sauté until translucent, about 5 minutes.
2. Add minced garlic and grated ginger to the pot. Sauté for another 1-2 minutes until fragrant.
3. Add diced pumpkin to the pot. Cook, stirring occasionally, for about 5 minutes.
4. Pour in vegetable or chicken broth and bring to a boil. Reduce heat to medium-low and simmer for 20-25 minutes, or until pumpkin is tender.
5. Using an immersion blender, blend the soup until smooth. If you don't have an immersion blender, carefully transfer the soup in batches to a blender and blend until smooth.
6. Stir in coconut milk, honey or maple syrup (if using), ground cinnamon, and ground nutmeg. Simmer for another 5 minutes, stirring occasionally.
7. Season with salt and pepper to taste.
8. Serve hot, garnished with chopped fresh cilantro or parsley.

Enjoy your creamy and comforting ginger pumpkin soup! It pairs wonderfully with crusty bread or a simple salad for a complete meal. Adjust the sweetness and spices according to your taste preferences for a perfect bowl of soup.

Lemon Fish Soup

Ingredients:

- 1 lb white fish fillets (such as cod or tilapia), cut into bite-sized pieces
- 6 cups fish or chicken broth
- 1/2 cup long-grain white rice
- 3 eggs
- Juice of 2 lemons
- Salt and pepper, to taste
- Fresh dill, chopped, for garnish

Instructions:

1. In a large pot, bring fish or chicken broth to a boil over medium-high heat.
2. Add long-grain white rice to the pot. Reduce heat to medium-low and simmer for 15-20 minutes, or until rice is tender.
3. Add white fish fillets to the pot. Simmer for another 5-7 minutes, or until fish is cooked through and flakes easily with a fork.
4. In a bowl, whisk together eggs and lemon juice until well combined.
5. Gradually ladle about 1 cup of hot broth from the pot into the egg-lemon mixture, whisking constantly to temper the eggs.
6. Slowly pour the egg-lemon mixture back into the pot, stirring gently to combine. Be careful not to boil the soup at this stage to prevent curdling.
7. Season with salt and pepper to taste.
8. Serve hot, garnished with chopped fresh dill.

Enjoy your tangy and comforting lemon fish soup! It's a refreshing dish with a unique texture and flavor profile that makes it perfect for any occasion. Adjust the amount of lemon juice according to your taste preferences for a more or less tangy soup.

Minestrone

Ingredients:

- 2 tbsp olive oil
- 1 onion, diced
- 2 cloves garlic, minced
- 2 carrots, diced
- 2 celery stalks, diced
- 1 zucchini, diced
- 1 yellow squash, diced
- 1 cup green beans, trimmed and cut into 1-inch pieces
- 1 can (14 oz) diced tomatoes
- 6 cups vegetable or chicken broth
- 1 can (15 oz) kidney beans, drained and rinsed
- 1 can (15 oz) cannellini beans, drained and rinsed
- 1 cup small pasta (such as ditalini or small shells)
- 1 tsp dried oregano
- 1 tsp dried basil
- Salt and pepper, to taste
- Fresh parsley or basil, chopped, for garnish
- Grated Parmesan cheese, for serving (optional)

Instructions:

1. Heat olive oil in a large pot over medium heat. Add diced onion and sauté until translucent, about 5 minutes.
2. Add minced garlic and sauté for another minute until fragrant.
3. Add diced carrots, celery, zucchini, yellow squash, and green beans to the pot. Cook for about 5 minutes, stirring occasionally.
4. Stir in diced tomatoes (with their juices) and vegetable or chicken broth. Bring to a boil.
5. Reduce heat to medium-low. Add drained and rinsed kidney beans and cannellini beans to the pot. Simmer for 15-20 minutes, or until vegetables are tender.
6. Stir in small pasta and dried herbs (oregano, basil). Continue to simmer for another 10-12 minutes, or until pasta is al dente.
7. Season with salt and pepper to taste.
8. Serve hot, garnished with chopped fresh parsley or basil. Optionally, sprinkle with grated Parmesan cheese.

This minestrone soup is hearty, nutritious, and perfect for any time of the year. Feel free to adjust the vegetables and herbs according to your preference. Enjoy with crusty bread or a side salad for a complete meal!

Outback Oxtail Soup

Ingredients:

- 2 lbs oxtails, trimmed of excess fat
- 2 tbsp olive oil
- 1 onion, chopped
- 2 carrots, diced
- 2 celery stalks, diced
- 2 cloves garlic, minced
- 1 tbsp tomato paste
- 6 cups beef broth
- 1 cup red wine (optional)
- 2 bay leaves
- 1 tsp dried thyme
- 1 tsp dried rosemary
- Salt and pepper, to taste
- Fresh parsley, chopped, for garnish

Instructions:

1. In a large pot or Dutch oven, heat olive oil over medium-high heat. Add oxtails and brown them on all sides, about 5-7 minutes. Remove oxtails and set aside.
2. In the same pot, add chopped onion, diced carrots, and diced celery. Sauté until vegetables are softened, about 5 minutes.
3. Add minced garlic and tomato paste to the pot. Cook for another 1-2 minutes until fragrant.
4. Return browned oxtails to the pot. Pour in beef broth and red wine (if using). Bring to a boil.
5. Reduce heat to low. Add bay leaves, dried thyme, and dried rosemary to the pot. Season with salt and pepper to taste.
6. Cover and simmer gently for 2.5 to 3 hours, or until the oxtails are tender and meat is falling off the bones. Skim off any foam or fat that rises to the surface during cooking.
7. Remove oxtails from the pot and let them cool slightly. Remove meat from the bones, shred or chop into bite-sized pieces, and discard bones and any excess fat.
8. Return shredded oxtail meat to the pot. Adjust seasoning if needed.
9. Serve hot, garnished with chopped fresh parsley.

Enjoy your hearty Outback oxtail soup! This comforting dish pairs well with crusty bread or a side salad for a satisfying meal. Adjust the cooking time if necessary to ensure the oxtails are tender and the flavors are well-developed.

Saltbush Soup

Ingredients:

- 1 bunch of saltbush leaves, washed and chopped (about 2 cups)
- 2 tbsp olive oil
- 1 onion, chopped
- 2 cloves garlic, minced
- 2 potatoes, peeled and diced
- 4 cups vegetable or chicken broth
- 1 cup milk or cream
- Salt and pepper, to taste
- Fresh parsley, chopped, for garnish

Instructions:

1. Heat olive oil in a large pot over medium heat. Add chopped onion and sauté until translucent, about 5 minutes.
2. Add minced garlic and sauté for another minute until fragrant.
3. Add diced potatoes to the pot and cook for about 5 minutes, stirring occasionally.
4. Add chopped saltbush leaves to the pot and sauté for another 2-3 minutes.
5. Pour in vegetable or chicken broth. Bring to a boil, then reduce heat to medium-low and simmer for 15-20 minutes, or until potatoes are tender.
6. Using an immersion blender, blend the soup until smooth. Alternatively, transfer the soup in batches to a blender and blend until smooth, then return to the pot.
7. Stir in milk or cream to achieve desired consistency. Simmer for another 5 minutes, stirring occasionally.
8. Season with salt and pepper to taste.
9. Serve hot, garnished with chopped fresh parsley.

Enjoy your flavorful Saltbush Soup! This soup showcases the unique taste of saltbush leaves, complemented by creamy potatoes and savory broth. It's perfect for a comforting meal, especially if you're exploring Australian culinary ingredients. Adjust the seasoning and consistency according to your preference for a delicious bowl of soup.

Thai Fish Soup

Ingredients:

- 1 lb white fish fillets (such as cod or tilapia), cut into bite-sized pieces
- 4 cups fish or chicken broth
- 2 stalks lemongrass, bruised and chopped into 2-inch pieces
- 3-4 kaffir lime leaves, torn
- 2-3 red chilies, sliced (adjust to taste)
- 1-inch piece of galangal or ginger, sliced
- 1 small onion, sliced
- 1 tomato, cut into wedges
- 1 cup mushrooms (straw mushrooms or button mushrooms), sliced
- 2 tbsp fish sauce
- 1 tbsp soy sauce
- 1 tbsp palm sugar or brown sugar
- Juice of 1-2 limes
- Fresh cilantro or Thai basil, chopped, for garnish
- Fresh chili slices, for garnish (optional)

Instructions:

1. In a large pot, bring fish or chicken broth to a boil over medium-high heat.
2. Add lemongrass, kaffir lime leaves, red chilies, galangal or ginger, and onion to the pot. Simmer for 5-7 minutes to infuse flavors.
3. Add sliced tomatoes, mushrooms, fish sauce, soy sauce, and palm sugar (or brown sugar) to the pot. Stir to combine.
4. Add white fish fillets to the pot. Cook for 3-5 minutes, or until fish is cooked through and flakes easily with a fork.
5. Remove from heat and stir in lime juice. Taste and adjust seasoning with more fish sauce, lime juice, or sugar as needed.
6. Serve hot, garnished with fresh cilantro or Thai basil, and optional chili slices for extra heat.

Enjoy your spicy and aromatic Thai fish soup! It's a comforting and flavorful dish that showcases the vibrant flavors of Thai cuisine. Adjust the level of spiciness by adding more or less chili according to your taste preferences. Serve with steamed rice for a complete meal.

Warrigal Greens Soup

Ingredients:

- 1 bunch Warrigal greens, washed and chopped (about 4 cups)
- 2 tbsp olive oil
- 1 onion, chopped
- 2 cloves garlic, minced
- 2 potatoes, peeled and diced
- 4 cups vegetable or chicken broth
- 1 cup milk or cream
- Salt and pepper, to taste
- Fresh lemon juice, to taste
- Fresh parsley, chopped, for garnish

Instructions:

1. Heat olive oil in a large pot over medium heat. Add chopped onion and sauté until translucent, about 5 minutes.
2. Add minced garlic and sauté for another minute until fragrant.
3. Add diced potatoes to the pot and cook for about 5 minutes, stirring occasionally.
4. Add chopped Warrigal greens to the pot and sauté for another 2-3 minutes.
5. Pour in vegetable or chicken broth. Bring to a boil, then reduce heat to medium-low and simmer for 15-20 minutes, or until potatoes are tender.
6. Using an immersion blender, blend the soup until smooth. Alternatively, transfer the soup in batches to a blender and blend until smooth, then return to the pot.
7. Stir in milk or cream to achieve desired consistency. Simmer for another 5 minutes, stirring occasionally.
8. Season with salt, pepper, and fresh lemon juice to taste.
9. Serve hot, garnished with chopped fresh parsley.

Enjoy your nutritious and flavorful Warrigal Greens Soup! This soup highlights the unique taste of Warrigal greens, complemented by creamy potatoes and savory broth. It's a comforting and wholesome dish, perfect for exploring Australian culinary ingredients. Adjust the seasoning and consistency according to your preference for a delicious bowl of soup.

Zucchini and Parmesan Soup

Ingredients:

- 2 tbsp olive oil
- 1 onion, chopped
- 2 cloves garlic, minced
- 4 medium zucchini, diced
- 4 cups vegetable or chicken broth
- 1 cup grated Parmesan cheese
- 1/2 cup heavy cream (optional)
- Salt and pepper, to taste
- Fresh basil leaves, chopped, for garnish

Instructions:

1. Heat olive oil in a large pot over medium heat. Add chopped onion and sauté until translucent, about 5 minutes.
2. Add minced garlic and sauté for another minute until fragrant.
3. Add diced zucchini to the pot and cook for about 5-7 minutes, until softened.
4. Pour in vegetable or chicken broth. Bring to a boil, then reduce heat to medium-low and simmer for 15-20 minutes, or until zucchini is tender.
5. Using an immersion blender, blend the soup until smooth. Alternatively, transfer the soup in batches to a blender and blend until smooth, then return to the pot.
6. Stir in grated Parmesan cheese until melted and well combined. If using, add heavy cream for extra richness.
7. Season with salt and pepper to taste.
8. Serve hot, garnished with chopped fresh basil leaves and an extra sprinkle of Parmesan cheese if desired.

Enjoy your creamy and comforting zucchini and Parmesan soup! It's a perfect dish to showcase the flavors of fresh zucchini and the nuttiness of Parmesan cheese. Serve with crusty bread or a side salad for a complete meal. Adjust the consistency by adding more broth or cream according to your preference.

Lemon Chicken Soup

Ingredients:

- 4 cups chicken broth
- 1 cup cooked chicken breast, shredded or diced
- 1/2 cup white rice
- 2 eggs
- Juice of 2 lemons
- Salt and pepper, to taste
- Fresh parsley, chopped, for garnish

Instructions:

1. In a large pot, bring chicken broth to a boil over medium-high heat.
2. Add white rice to the pot. Reduce heat to medium-low and simmer for 15-20 minutes, or until rice is tender.
3. Stir in cooked chicken breast to the pot. Simmer for another 5 minutes to heat through.
4. In a bowl, whisk together eggs and lemon juice until well combined.
5. Gradually ladle about 1 cup of hot broth from the pot into the egg-lemon mixture, whisking constantly to temper the eggs.
6. Slowly pour the egg-lemon mixture back into the pot, stirring gently to combine. Be careful not to boil the soup at this stage to prevent curdling.
7. Season with salt and pepper to taste.
8. Serve hot, garnished with chopped fresh parsley.

Enjoy your delicious and tangy lemon chicken soup! It's a comforting dish that balances the richness of chicken with the bright flavor of lemon. Serve with crusty bread or a side salad for a complete meal. Adjust the lemon juice according to your taste preferences for a more or less tangy soup.

Beetroot and Feta Soup

Ingredients:

- 4 medium-sized beetroots, peeled and diced
- 1 onion, chopped
- 2 cloves garlic, minced
- 4 cups vegetable or chicken broth
- 1/2 cup feta cheese, crumbled
- 1/4 cup plain Greek yogurt (optional, for creaminess)
- 2 tbsp olive oil
- Salt and pepper, to taste
- Fresh dill, chopped, for garnish

Instructions:

1. Heat olive oil in a large pot over medium heat. Add chopped onion and sauté until translucent, about 5 minutes.
2. Add minced garlic and sauté for another minute until fragrant.
3. Add diced beetroots to the pot and cook for about 5 minutes, stirring occasionally.
4. Pour in vegetable or chicken broth. Bring to a boil, then reduce heat to medium-low and simmer for 20-25 minutes, or until beetroots are tender.
5. Using an immersion blender, blend the soup until smooth. Alternatively, transfer the soup in batches to a blender and blend until smooth, then return to the pot.
6. Stir in crumbled feta cheese until melted and well combined. If using, stir in plain Greek yogurt for extra creaminess.
7. Season with salt and pepper to taste.
8. Serve hot, garnished with chopped fresh dill.

Enjoy your creamy and flavorful beetroot and feta soup! It's a vibrant and nutritious dish that pairs well with crusty bread or a side salad. Adjust the consistency by adding more broth or yogurt according to your preference.

www.ingramcontent.com/pod-product-compliance
Lightning Source LLC
LaVergne TN
LVHW061953070526
838199LV00060B/4090